How To Box
By: Joe Louis

ISBN: 978-1-63923-448-6

Printed: June 2022

Cover Art By: Amit Paul

Published and Distributed By:
Lushena Books
607 Country Club Drive, Unit E
Bensenville, IL 60106
www.lushenabooksinc.com/books

ISBN: 978-1-63923-448-6

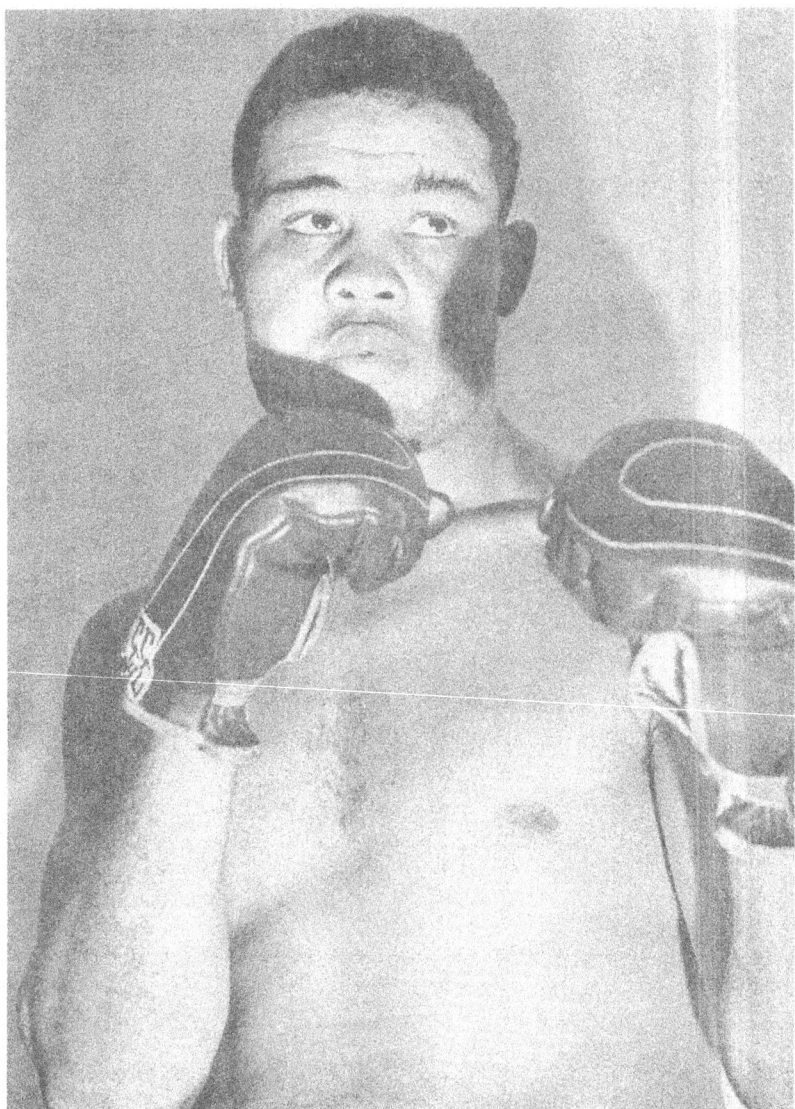

I GUESS THIS IS HOW I LOOK AT FIRST TO WHOEVER'S FIGHTING ME.

HOW

to

BOX

by

JOE
LOUIS

Edited by
EDWARD J. MALLORY

I'D RATHER PUNCH A BAG, OR JOE WALCOTT, THAN HAVE TO PUNCH THIS.

ALL PHOTOGRAPHS FROM INTERNATIONAL NEWS PHOTOS
DRAWINGS BY JAMES LEONARD
LAYOUT BY HERBERT BENDER

THIS EDITION IS PRINTED IN ENGLAND
BY
DRYDENS PRINTERS LIMITED
LONDON   N. W. 10

CONTENTS

ME IN 1936 BEFORE THE FIRST SCHMELING BOUT, WHEN I NEEDED SOME LESSONS MYSELF.

FOREWORD

JOE LOUIS is the greatest boxing champion of all times. By June, 1948, he had been heavyweight champion of the world for eleven years, setting an all time record. During these eleven years, he has been the idol of the sports world. He has defended his title twenty-three times; always exemplifying true sportsmanship. He has met all aspirants, and even given worthy ones a second chance to win his title.

When Joe felt that Uncle Sam needed his strength and power to fight for his country, he was among the first to volunteer. His comment made at that time, "we'll win because we're on God's side," will never be forgotten.

The youth of the world have acclaimed Joe Louis their favourite personality. He, in turn, has given a perfect example of true heroism. He has been commended for his honesty, loyalty, utter simplicity, and profound dignity, always shown both in and out of the ring. It is to these youths that Joe wishes to dedicate this book, hoping that it may, in some small way, help them to become future champions of the world.

7

I HOPE I NEVER LET DOWN KIDS WHO LOOK UP TO ME. (TAKEN IN BOSTON.)

MIND DISCIPLINE

FROM CHILDHOOD it is necessary to train your mind with clean thoughts, free of all hatreds and fears, if not you will be seriously hampered in your efforts to learn to box. Blood pressure, nerve tension and other bodily conditions are harmfully affected by a bad mental attitude. Anger, kept in your heart, burns up your nerves and your energy, which are both important in conditioning.

The strict discipline needed in training will require giving up many things: ease, comfort and all forms of dissipation. You must learn to follow rules and regulations and to always respect the other fellow. You must be able to take reverses and not become sour. You must become more tolerant and more patient than others; and above all you must have the will and determination to succeed.

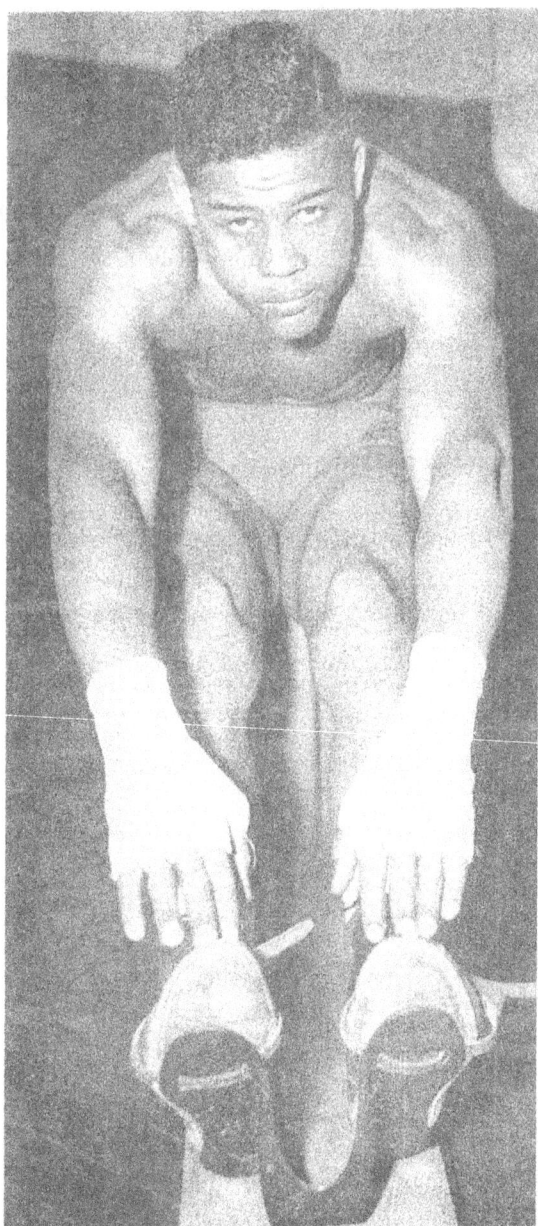

ELEMENTARY TRAINING

THE SOLID FOUNDATION of good health to train and box successfully is based primarily on proper diet and rest. Food is important not only to keep you alive; but to give you the necessary energy needed for boxing. Proteins such as fish, meats, eggs, milk and cheese are tissue builders. Carbohydrates such as bread, cereals and sugar produce energy. Calcium, found in milk, will build strong bones and teeth. Lean meats, milk, fruit and leafy vegetables are particularly good during training. Glucose candy is also very good because of its sugar content.

Plenty of water used internally and externally is very important. With the correct food and exercise, you should have no trouble with proper elimination. There should be absolutely no smoking or alcoholic beverages allowed.

A boxer needs plenty of sleep because he is exercising strenuously during training, which breaks down the cells and uses stored-up energy. Remember, you cannot catch up on sleep, so it is necessary to get eight to ten hours each night in a well ventilated room.

11

LIMBERING UP, BEFORE STARTING TO SPAR
AT POMPTON LAKES, N.J. TRAINING CAMP.
MY HANDS HAVE BEEN BANDAGED FOR
THE SPARRING GLOVES, AS YOU CAN SEE.

EQUIPMENT

IN THE PRESENT DAY of boxing you will find most cities have either a Y.M.C.A., Boys Club, or regular Gymnasiums fitted with facilities for the amateur or professional boxer. They should be equipped with light and heavy punching bags, exercise mats, and wall pulleys; with, of course, a boxing ring.

The hands must be wrapped correctly when punching or striking in any manner to protect you from breaking or injuring the hand. My advice would be to have an expert trainer to wrap them first, and after learning yourself, make sure not to get the gauze too tight. It might stop the circulation in your hands.

There are four sets of gloves used by a boxer. The fourteen ounce glove, which is used in training and exhibitions. The light glove used for punching the light bag; the heavy gloves for punching the heavy bag; and six ounce gloves for actual fighting.

The headgear for boxers is used in training to prevent injuries to the eyes and ears.

The rubber mouthpiece should be made by your dentist, to insure proper fit and to protect breaking of the teeth and cutting lips.

The athletic supporter should be the aluminium cup type, which protects against injuries from accidental fouls.

White wool socks should be worn with soft soled shoes, to prevent slipping.

Other important items are sterilized sponge, clean towels and soap, personal water bottle, separate buckets for sponge and ice bag, and medical kit. To have these personal items will help eliminate germs.

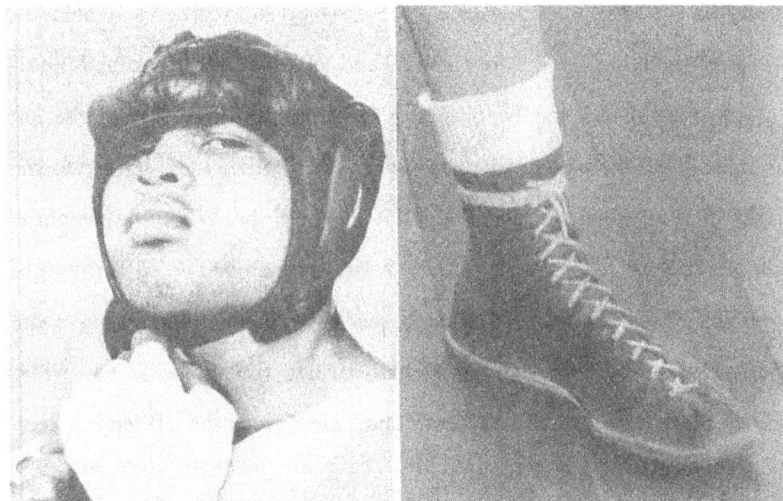

MY HEADGEAR AND MY FOOTWEAR FOR MY TRAINING. MY FEET ARE SHOD THE SAME WAY IN A CHAMPIONSHIP FIGHT. SHOESTRINGS MUSTN'T COME UNDONE OR BREAK.

THE PROPER STANCE

BOXING IS BASICALLY BUILT on punching and footwork, and before doing either correctly it is necessary to have the proper stance. For effective punching the weight must be shifted from one leg to the other. Improper movements of the feet can lose a bout. The position of the feet is important for maintaining balance; they should be directly under the body about medium distance apart. This position gives you balance, speed, relaxation, easy movements, and great power for punching.

Proper stance can be obtained by stepping forward with the left foot, shifting the weight on that foot. Turn the left toes slightly to the right, making sure the left foot is flat on the floor. When the weight is shifted to the left leg, the right heel raises an inch or two with the right toes pointing forward. If stance is too narrow for balance, move the right foot a few inches to the right to widen the stance; if too wide, glide the right foot forward a few inches. Don't lock the left leg but keep it straight.

The left arm is crooked, with the elbow down in front of the left ribs. The left hand should be shoulder high, about one foot away from the left shoulder. The left hand is closed; but not too tightly, with the thumb side up and with the knuckles pointing outside.

WITH THIS STANCE YOU'RE READY TO
DEFEND OR ATTACK. THIS IS THE 4TH
ROUND OF THE CONN FIGHT IN 1946.

SHOWING THE STANCE AGAIN, FEET SET FOR POWER PUNCHING.

THE PROPER STANCE

The right arm is crooked, with the elbow directly down in front of the right ribs. The right hand is opened slightly pointing toward the opponent about four inches from the right shoulder. Both arms should be relaxed and easy to assure readiness to attack or to defend.

The head should have no singular action of its own; it works along with the body. The chin should always be pinned down on the chest bone. Any other position of the chin will cause unnecessary tiredness and will leave you open for your opponent's blow.

To find out if you have the proper stance try these exercises:

1—Bend backward and forward from the hips, bending the knees at the same time; this is similar to weaving.

2—Raise up on the balls of the feet, spring down in a squatting position and up again. Sway from side to side and without moving your feet, bend forward.

If these exercises can be performed without losing your balance, you have the proper stance.

CORRECT PUNCHING

CORRECT PUNCHING demands careful study and practice to perfect. Powerful punching does not derive from just the hands and arms; but from the body when properly used. Use the weight of your body in every punch, and the arms as a transmitter. Punching straight from the shoulder means the weight shifted so that the hips and shoulder lead the arm to the centre of the object.

The quickest and easiest exercise to learn to punch correctly, is to lift the right foot off the floor; now let go with a right hand punch to the bag. The body weight must lead the punch because there is no brace by the right foot to hold back the weight. You will get full power punches very quickly. You must alternate punches. Practise daily until your body power is in all your punches. Remember to punch straight forward and don't swing or sway to get best results.

The correct way to make a fist so as not to break any bones of the hand when punching, is to fold the fingers in the palm of the hand and close the thumb across the second and third fingers making the thumb side of the hand flat.

Always move in towards your opponent when punching.

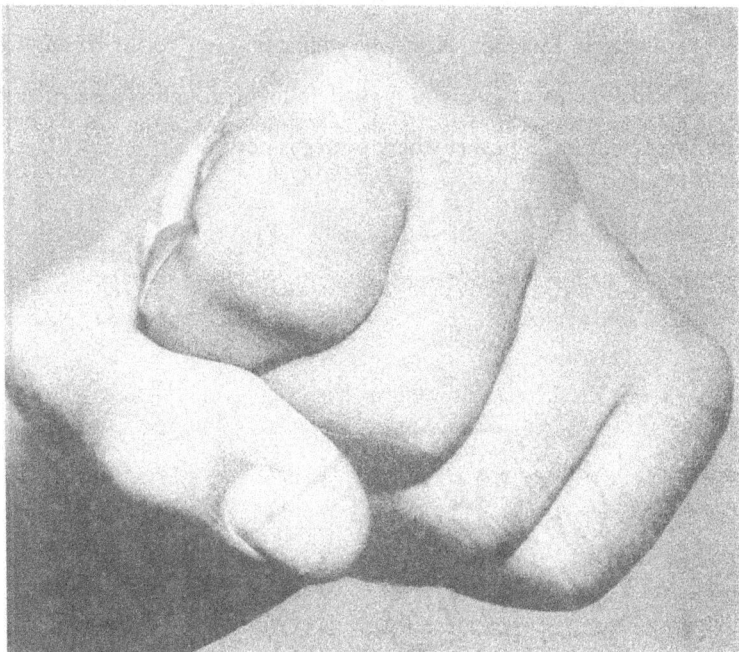

IF YOU COULD SEE MY FIST THROUGH THE BANDAGES AND THE GLOVE WHEN I GET TO WORK WITH IT IN A FIGHT, IT'D LOOK LIKE THIS, WITH LEATHER BETWEEN THUMB AND FINGERS.

Standing in the proper stance and turning the body quickly to the left, shooting the right hand out straight to the chin without taking a step, can cause a quick knockout. Alternate and practise this exercise in front of a mirror daily. This will enable you to master quick, powerful punches, which are needed in gaining points.

As in golf and baseball, it is necessary at all times to keep the left side of the body and the left leg in a straight line. This will insure the proper power in punches. Also when punching, try to hit through the target, which helps to give you a good follow through. These rules are very important in any sport where power is needed.

MY FIGHTING FIST (RIGHT HAND) FROM THE INSIDE.

FOOTWORK

FOOTWORK is an important part of boxing. You must be able to move the body easily at all times so that balance will not be disturbed. Knowing when and where to move is the foundation of great skill in boxing. Clever footwork does not mean hopping and jumping around, as this will put you off balance and the slightest blow will upset you. The purpose of clever footwork is to give your opponent false leads and to tire him by making him hit at the wrong target. It also carries you out of danger when hurt.

There are basically four movements in footwork: forward movement; backward movement; circling left; and circling right.

The forward movement is a slow shuffle or a quick movement of a few inches at a time leading with the left foot with the right foot following, always maintaining the proper stance throughout the movement. The knees are not rigid, but feel loose and free during the slightest movement. The left foot is flat on the floor, and the right toes are firm on the floor. Important to remember is to always slide the feet along the floor, and keep the proper stance when moving forward.

The backward movement is the same as the forward movement, except that you should slide the right foot a couple of inches backward

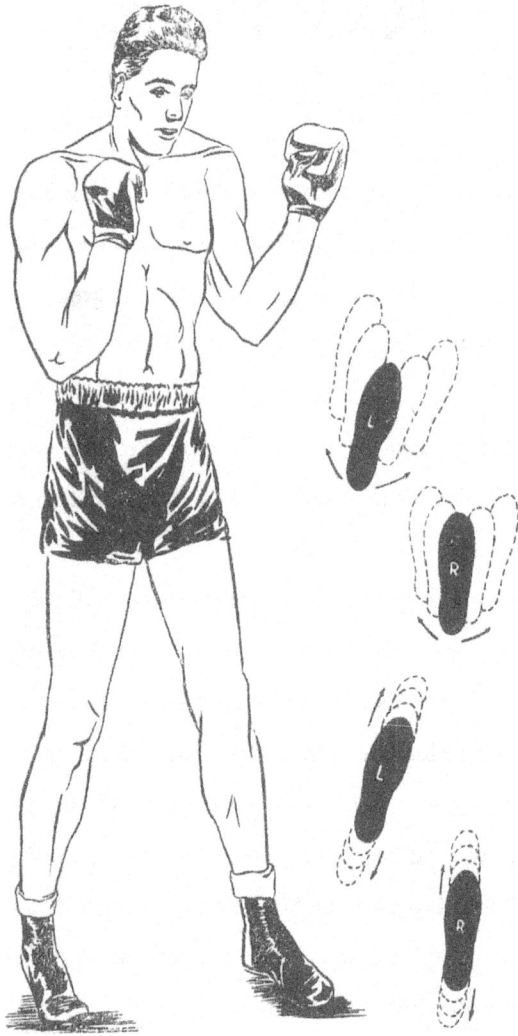

GOOD FOOTWORK TO KEEP YOUR OPPONENT OFF BALANCE.

FOOTWORK

followed by the left foot. Always remember to maintain the proper stance.

Circling left is a gliding step to the left, leading with the left foot, with the right foot following. The proper stance is always maintained throughout these movements. When leading with the left foot there is no given distance of how short or how long to step; but always make sure you keep your balance.

Circling right is a gliding step to the right, moving the left foot towards the right foot and then moving the right foot into the proper stance.

You should always move in the opposite direction of your opponent's strongest and best blow, never crossing your feet, and always be in position to defend yourself or to attack your opponent.

PUNCHING THE BAG

BEFORE ATTEMPTING to punch the bag at all, make sure that your hands have been properly bandaged by an expert. The bandage should never be placed between the fingers, as this will spread the bones of the hand. You should close your hands several times during the bandaging to make sure it is not stopping the blood circulation. After the hands are bandaged, proper gloves are put on, and always remember your thumb is to hold the glove tight on the hand, not to punch with as it is too easily injured.

There are two bags used in training; the light bag and the heavy bag. The light bag helps you develop blows to the head and trains your eyes to measure a bobbing target accurately. It also helps to develop the muscles of the arms, shoulders, neck, wrists and legs.

The light bag should be the same height as your chin so that you can aim straight instead of bringing your punches up to meet the bag. After doing this well, you should raise and lower the bag so that you may practise hitting a shorter or taller opponent than you are.

Stand directly in front of the bag, sway your body to the left until your right hand will be directly in front of bag when brought up. Hit the bag with the face of the fist as it is going away from you. Then sway to the right and practise with your left hand. The quickest way to learn how to punch the bag is to remember you must start slowly and keep it up until you gain self confidence and then you will begin to pick up speed without realizing it.

The heavy bag is used for learning how to deliver the various blows. The bag is hung so that the bottom is on the level with your hips, so that you won't hit lower than the belt or waistline. Assume the proper stance and start hitting out straight just as you would at an opponent. You will note from the feel of the fist whether you are hitting correctly or if you are getting the maximum power behind the blow. If one knuckle is hitting harder than the other, or the thumb is striking the bag, you are hitting wrong, so start punching slower to observe what is wrong.

After learning to hit the bag while it is stationary, try giving it a slight push to start it slowly swinging. Then when it has started to swing away, hook sharply with the left or right in the direction of the swing of the bag. This is good practice as it accustoms you to hitting the side of an opponent who turns from a blow.

The heavy bag is also used to develop rapid hitting to the body, which is called in-fighting. Crouch slightly forward with both feet in line together, and bring both hands upward in sharp, short blows to the bag. Treat the bag as you would your opponent. If the bag gives way, assume your opponent is retreating from your attack, step closer and continue punching away with both hands. Then assume that your opponent is holding, back away but quickly return to the attack with both hands. This will help you to get more power behind your blows and teach you to stay in close, so that your opponent's blows are robbed of their force.

Punching the heavy bag should be timed into rounds, three minutes of punching with one minute of rest in between.

SESSIONS WITH THE PUNCH BALL OR BAG HELP TUNE UP YOUR FOOTWORK, TOO. THE BAG KEEPS YOU SHIFTING YOUR WEIGHT AROUND A GOOD DEAL LIKE YOU MUST WHEN FACING AN OPPONENT IN THE RING.

TRAINING

EVERY BOXER that has ever won a fight has done so by conscientious and faithful training. You should start by doing a few exercises each day until you are able to do all those that are necessary without becoming too tired or taxing your physical resources. The amount of training depends on each individual's needs; it is never wise to over train, and moderation should be followed in all exercises.

Roadwork is very good for strengthening the legs, increasing lung power and strengthening the heart; however, it should not be overdone as it will then do more harm than good. Never run until you become too tired or exhausted. It is best to maintain a steady pace in your road runs, breathing deeply and evenly. Many boxers run the same length of time as they box, resting one minute between each three minute session. To sharpen your mind, you should sprint for two hundred yards, then walk for one hundred yards to regain your measured steady breathing before sprinting again. You should never run for at least three or four hours after eating. When walking or running you should carry a small, very soft rubber ball in each hand and squeeze them as they will aid in strengthening the muscles of the fingers and the wrists.

Skipping rope is another training exercise which should be done as

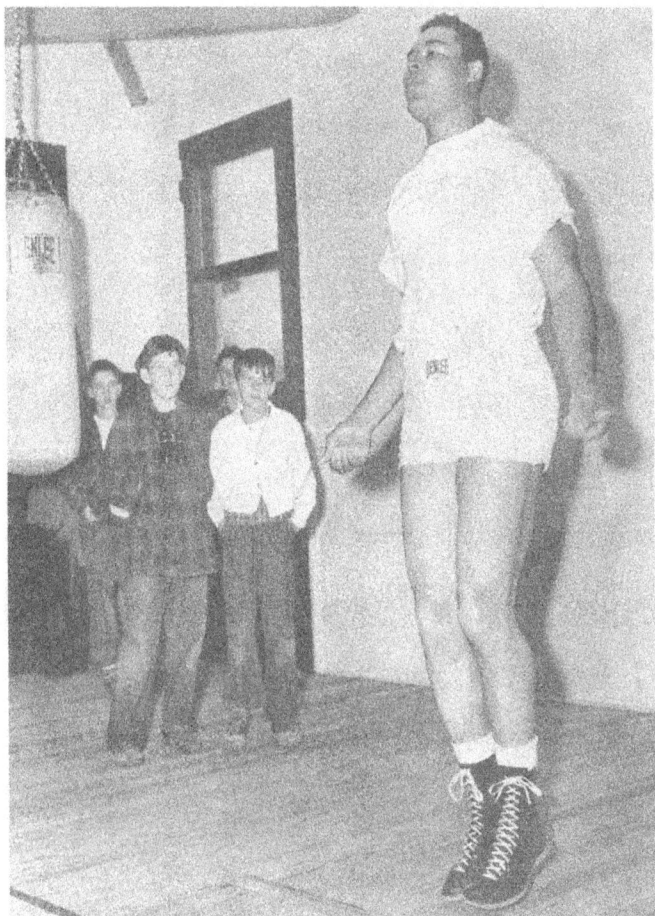

I GUESS AS A KID I THOUGHT SKIPPING-THE-ROPE WAS KINDA SISSY. NOW I KNOW IT'S A GOOD EXERCISE FOR ANYBODY. NOTHING'S BETTER FOR GETTING LEGS IN SPRINGY SHAPE.

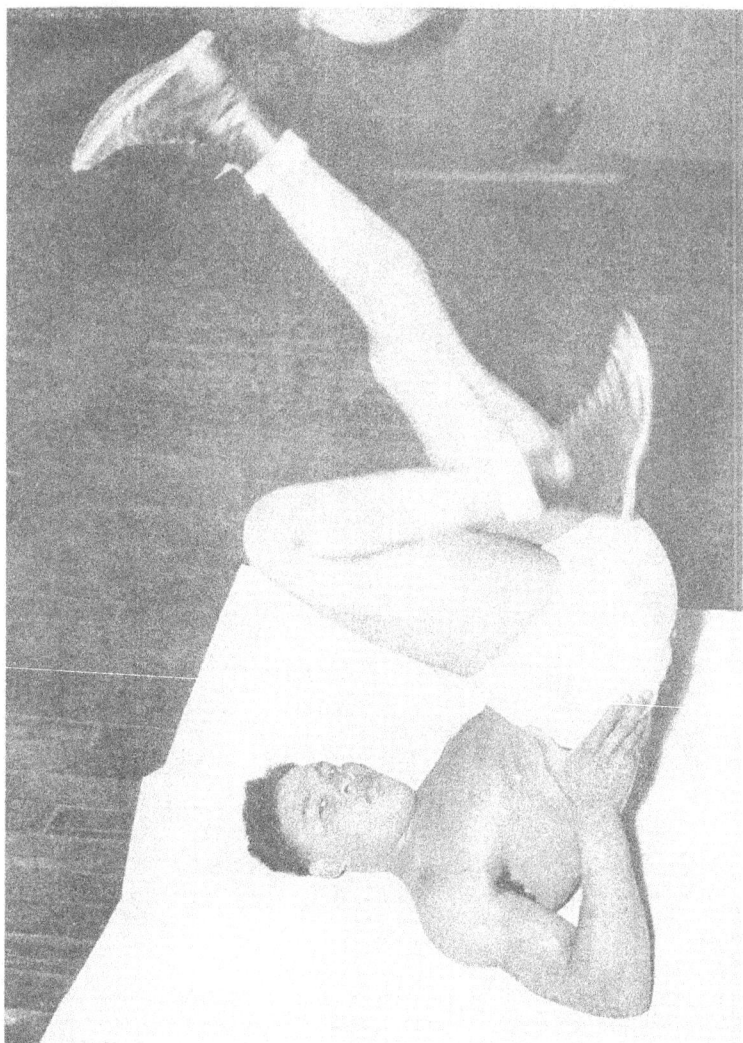

IN THIS EXERCISE, TO LIMBER UP LEG MUSCLES, YOU MOVE YOUR LEGS
UP AND DOWN AND AROUND AS IF PEDALLING A BIKE A MILE OR TWO.

your boxing, three minutes to a round and then rest one minute. It is helpful in developing better foot movements and in limbering up the muscles of the biceps, wrists and shoulders.

Shadow boxing is used to perfect boxing skill and to acquire ring form. Stand before a mirror and try shadow boxing if you are not sure you are using the correct form for a certain blow. Shadow box just as you would actually box, always punching hard and timing yourself to three minute rounds.

The light and heavy bags should be used daily in training as explained in a previous chapter.

The pulley weights are very good to loosen and stretch all the muscles of the body. Shadow box facing the pulleys and then with your back to them, according to that three minute round routine.

The abdominal muscles are strengthened by lying flat on your back, raising and lowering your legs and going through the motions of riding a bicycle. Bring your knees close to your chest and have your trainer toss a medicine ball at your feet, which you return by striking the ball with the soles of your feet and kicking straight out. Another good exercise is to lie flat on your back, raise both legs together and make a complete circle, low and wide.

Finish your training period by boxing three or four rounds, and if possible with different sparring partners. Try to learn something from each partner. When finished, take a hot shower and then a cold shower, followed by a brisk rub with a coarse towel.

While training, you should sleep in a well ventilated room getting at least ten hours sleep daily. Drink plenty of water; but never with meals. Your diet should consist of plenty of fruits, vegetables and lean meats. If trying to lose weight, omit all starches. Never at any time wear anything with rubber to help reduce, instead during exercises wear an undershirt, long drawers and a white sweat shirt. After exercising, lie down with clothes off with a heavy woollen blanket around you for twenty minutes, and when thoroughly dry, take a luke warm tub bath. Epsom salts baths are also very good with a doctor's consent. If trying to gain weight, include in your diet all starches and sugars which are flesh and energy building. Regular bowel movements are very important to your general health. A visit to your dentist, chiropodist, eye, and medical doctor should be made at least every three months. Above all, follow strictly all the rules given you by your trainer, if you hope to become successful.

MY SPARRING PARTNERS AREN'T JUST SET-UPS. (JOE WALCOTT USED TO BE ONE.) YOU HAVE TO HAVE REAL OPPOSITION IN TRAINING ROUNDS. THE BOY WITH ME HERE IS RAY WILLIAMS. I WAS GETTING THE RUST OUT OF THE SPRINGS OF MY TIMING OF LEFTS AND RIGHTS.

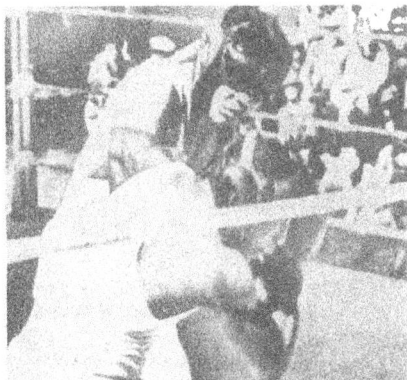

THE LEFT JAB
AND LEFT HOOK

THE LEFT JAB is seldom if ever a knockout blow; but many bouts are won by the skilful use of it. It is used to keep your opponent off balance and thus create openings for other more powerful blows. The left jab is a sharp thrust to the head or body of your opponent, never disturbing your body balance. From the proper stance, thrust your left fist aiming for the jaw or mouth, turn your body slightly to the right, and raise your right hand to guard against your opponent's blow. The power of the jab comes from the slight turning of the left shoulder to the right. Remembering to always jab through the mark and not at it, will give you the follow-through effect. Return your hand quickly to position for another jab, or to guard against your opponent's counter-attack.

The left hook is one of the most difficult blows to learn and use properly. The hook is used as a countering blow, and sometimes a finishing blow. The shorter this blow, the better the effect. The hook is used best against a left jab or a straight right as a counter blow. From the proper stance, and leaving the arm in that position, turn your body to the right, shifting your weight to the right leg, throw the left arm in an arc to the opponent's head. Make sure to hit through the mark and not

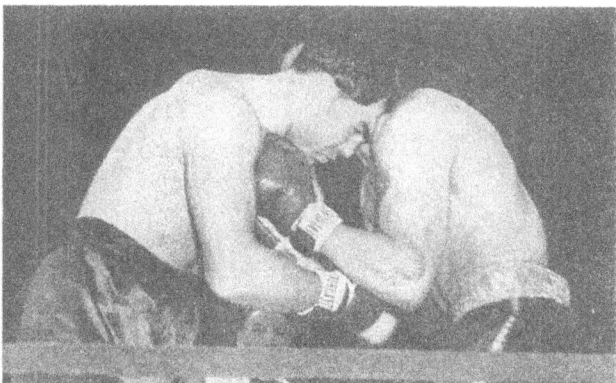

NOTHING GAVE ME MORE SATISFACTION THAN SINKING MY LEFT IN MAX SCHMELING'S JAW IN THAT ONE-ROUND RETURN BOUT—IN WHICH I KNOCKED HIM OUT.

SPEAKING OF LEFT JABS, HERE IS HOW I GAVE ONE TO BILLY CONN DURING THE FIRST FIGHT I HAD WITH HIM.

I GUESS ABOUT THE BEST WAY TO ILLUSTRATE THE RIGHT HOOK IS WITH THESE PICTURES TAKEN IN THE FOURTH ROUND OF THE FIGHT WITH TONY GAL-ENTO, IN JUNE 1939. GALENTO'S BODY HIDES THE BEGINNING OF THAT PUNCH WHICH FINISHED HIM. THE REFEREE YOU SEE IS ARTY DONOVAN.

just at it, with knuckles up at impact of blow. Practising the left hook will give you co-ordination of the body weight and the arm power, which brings about a snap in the blow, and gives more force. This hook can be practised on the heavy bag, starting slowly first, and picking up speed when you have reached the point of co-ordination.

It might be said at this time, that the left jab and left hook can readily be most effectively combined. In this use the left hook is a finishing blow, while the jab leads the combination. When you find an opponent whose right hand is slow in warding off the jab, this would be the appropriate time to jab him a couple of times, and then combine the jab and left hook, making them both in one motion.

This combination can also be used against an opponent who weaves, and sways his hands and body. You jab when his head is directly in front of you, and hook when the head returns back to where he started his weaving.

These are just a couple of spots to use this combination. After boxing and practising with different opponents you will find many more uses for the jab and left hook together.

"Two Ton" Tony Galento had me going and even knocked me down with a hard left in the third round. In the fourth, I threw a hard right to his jaw, then a powerful left hook which started his mouth, nose, and right eye bleeding. It seems I must have thrown a hundred hard punches to his head before he finally fell to his knees and the referee stopped the fight.

THE RIGHT CROSS

IN ORDER for the right cross to have the proper effect, it should be remembered that its success depends upon the speed with which it is carried out. Assuming the proper stance, bend your body slightly forward from the waist, then throwing your body power into it, bring your right arm up, over, and across (making almost a complete semi-circle) with all the strength and energy you possess. You should have landed your blow to the cheek or the jaw of your opponent with the full impact of your knuckles. If landed correctly and with the proper force, a powerful right cross will mean curtains for your opponent.

The left cross is carried out in the same way, reversing the entire action.

I guess in my second fight with Max Schmeling, I threw more punches in that one short round than I have ever done in such a short time. I tore into him with lefts and rights; but it was a short hard right

THESE ARE MORE PICTURES FROM THE ONE-ROUND SECOND BOUT WITH MAX SCHMELING. HE'S GOING DOWN UNDER RIGHT AND LEFT BODY SMASHES, FINISHED.

that really started his finish. I heard Max grunt and knew I had him. I staggered him with another hard right and he went down for the count of three. When he came up, I gave him another hard left and right and he was down again for the count of one. My last smashing right cross sent him to the canvas and this time his corner threw in the towel, making this the shortest fight of my career; exactly two minutes and four seconds of the first round.

THE STRAIGHT RIGHT

THE STRAIGHT RIGHT is one of the most dangerous blows in boxing. It is always preceded by a left lead and carries lots of force. To deliver a straight right to the chin, you must assume the proper stance, then shift your weight to the left leg and swing the right side of the body forward, driving your right fist straight out. Try to drive through your aim and not just at it. The left arm should be held close to the left side acting as guard. Then bring the right arm back to the proper stance.

A straight right to the body is delivered in the same way, except that the body is lowered forward from the waist before delivering the blow.

After a surprising right to my jaw thrown by Tami Mauriello, I moved in for the kill and sent him to the floor with a hard left hook for the count of nine. When he got up, after a left to the jaw and right to the body, I sent another left hook to his jaw and then a murderous straight right to the chin which dropped him in two minutes and nine seconds of the first round.

In the thirteenth round of my first fight with Conn, when Billy missed me with a zipping left hook, I quickly crossed a right to his jaw and followed it by several straight rights that sent him crashing to the canvas. I had to wait for Billy to miss and lose his head, as I knew I needed a knockout to win.

THE MAN ON THE RECEIVING END OF THIS RIGHT TO THE HEAD IS TAMI MAURIELLO

THE UPPERCUT

PERHAPS THE SHORTEST of all blows is the uppercut. In delivering a right uppercut, you assume the proper stance, facing your opponent, bend to the right and slightly forward, dropping your right arm a few inches and making sure that the fingers of your fist are facing your own body, bring your right arm up in an underhand arc to your opponent's chin. The slight twist that you give your right hip, as in the hook, will add plenty force to the blow. Often such a blow will send your opponent's body tumbling to the canvas.

The left uppercut is delivered in the same way except that the left side of the body is used instead of the right. During the delivery of an uppercut, your free arm should be held close to your chest and used as a guard.

In my second fight with Billy Conn, I set him up with several left jabs in the early rounds and after gaining an opening by using first a right cross and then a right uppercut, I let go a thunderous left hook that staggered him and sent him tumbling to the floor for the count.

SHOWING YOU HOW YOU START
THE RIGHT UPPERCUT WITH THE
PALM OF THE GLOVE UPPERMOST.
WEIGHT SHIFTS FROM THE RIGHT
TO THE LEFT WITH THE BLOW.

THE ONE TWO

STRIKING ONE BLOW and following it up by another blow is called "the one two." The two blows should be delivered swiftly and without any hesitation between blows. Assuming the proper stance, step forward with your left foot and deliver a left jab high enough to block your opponent's vision; follow immediately by a forward step with the right foot and deliver a forceful right blow to the chin. This action to be effective must be carried out with absolute precision and speed.

Many experts say "the one two" is delivered with the same hand, i.e., a right or left to jaw, then body ; or vice versa.

GIVING THE ONE-TWO TO SCHMELING. DO I SEEM TO HAVE A LOT OF PICTURES OF THAT SECOND BOUT? I LIKE TO SEE THEM !

LEFT ABOVE: FEINTING WITH MY LEFT AND JABBING ABE SIMON WITH MY RIGHT. RIGHT ABOVE: YOU SEE THE FOLLOW THROUGH AND THE EFFECT ON SIMON. LEFT BELOW: SIMON STAGGERS AND COLLIDES WITH MY LEFT. RIGHT BELOW: SIMON IS KNOCKED OUT, 6TH ROUND.

DEFENCE AND ATTACK

THE MOST IMPORTANT THING to learn in boxing is how to defend yourself and when to attack your opponent. There are various methods of defence including: ducking; blocking; parrying; slipping; clinching; weaving; side-stepping, and feinting.

Ducking is used when your opponent leads with a right or left to the chin; you should bend forward from the waist ducking his blow. As soon as you have ducked his blow, straighten up and at the same time counter with a blow to your opponent.

Blocking is used to protect the body and the chin from your opponent's blow. As your opponent leads, turn your body holding your elbow close to it, so that the blow is taken by the elbow. If your opponent should lead with a blow to the chin, use your shoulder to block it, by dropping your arm and turning your body enough so that your shoulder will receive the blow.

Parrying is used to ward off your opponent's blow just before it reaches its aim. As your opponent leads with a right or left, bring your opposite hand up and brush your opponent's blow outward, striking him on the wrist. Precision is more important than force.

Slipping is used against straight leads and counters. As your

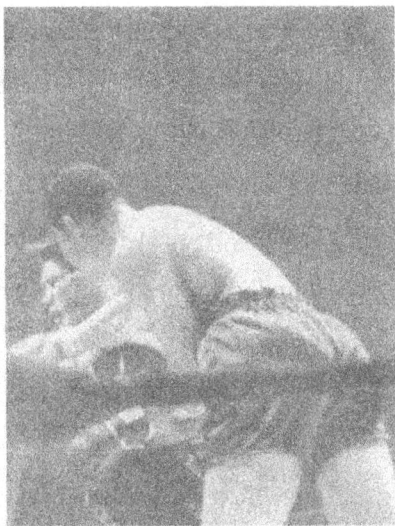

I'M DUCKING AND BLOCKING AS BILLY CONN TRIES TO REACH ME IN THE 13TH ROUND OF OUR FIRST FIGHT, IN 1941. THAT WAS THE FINAL ROUND OF THE BOUT; I KNOCKED HIM OUT.

opponent leads with his left, shift your body about five or six inches to the right of his blow, making it fall harmlessly over your shoulder and placing yourself in position for a left blow to his unprotected left side. Sometimes it is only necessary to move your head to "slip his punch."

Clinching is used when you are hurt, tired, after missing a blow, or when you hope to tire your opponent by superior weight and strength. Keeping your body very close to your opponent, move both hands downward from his shoulders, and holding his elbows stay in this position until the referee tells you to break.

Weaving is used to make your opponent miss by moving your upper trunk and head in a circular movement to the right or left. As your opponent leads with a blow, lower your head and body moving under his arm, straighten up and counter with a blow and then another as you continue to weave.

Sidestepping is used to avoid blows and create openings. As your opponent leads, you bring your left foot back so its toes are pointing towards the right heel, then take a step to the right, shifting your weight to the right leg while you twist your body at the waist away from his coming lead. By his blow missing you, he is off balance and open for your counter blow.

There are two basic methods of attack, either by force or by skill. The attack by force is used by the slugger who depends only on his hitting power. The attack by skill is used by the boxer who depends on his cleverness in feinting, correct leading, drawing and, infighting.

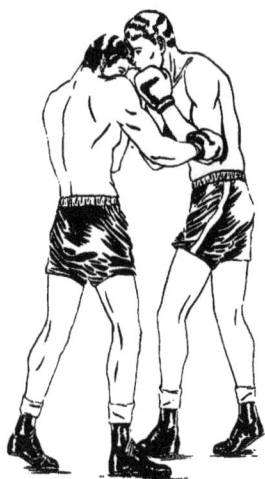

BLOCKING

PARRYING

SLIPPING

CLINCHING

WEAVING

SIDE-STEPPING

INFIGHTING

Feinting is used to deceive your opponent and put him off guard. It is the movement of some part of your body to give your opponent the impression that you intend to do one thing when you really intend to do something else. Assuming the proper stance, start a left jab to your opponent's chin, then just as he starts to ward off your blow, bring your left arm back and snap your right fist into his chin. Speed is very important to gain success in feinting. There are many popular feints such as: feint a straight right to the jaw and then hook a left to the body; feint a left jab to the stomach and then jab to the face; feint a right to the face and then jab a left to the chin; feint a left jab to the body and then a right uppercut to the chin. After lots of practice and some experience in boxing you will be able to think of many schemes to use in feinting.

Leading is always done by the left hand using the right hand as guard; except by southpaws, who would naturally lead with their right hand, using their left as guard.

Drawing is used when you want your opponent to deliver a specific blow, by leaving that particular part of your body momentarily exposed. This is done to create an opening for your attack.

Infighting is used to weaken your opponent by effective body punches. From the proper stance, draw a left lead from your opponent, then slipping inside and placing your head on his chest, push forward throwing him off balance. Then start a continuous peppering of blows to his body; this will weaken him so that after you have separated, your best blow will knock him to the canvas.

LEFT: FEELING OUT BRADDOCK IN THE FIRST ROUND
OF OUR FIGHT IN CHICAGO, 1937. BELOW, JIM
SLIPS PAST MY GUARD WITH A JOLTING LEFT. O
THE OPPOSITE PAGE: DUCKING UNDER JCE
WALCOTT'S RIGHT, I SHOOT OUT WITH MY OWN.

The most important fight of my entire career was on June 22nd, 1937, at Comiskey Park in Chicago, when I won the heavyweight title from James J. Braddock. In the early rounds if I hadn't side-stepped, weaved, and ducked a lot, one of those powerful rights he threw would have meant curtains for me. In the seventh, my hard lefts and rights started weakening him. Then in the eighth, after exchanging many lefts and rights, I connected with a terrific right to his jaw that sent him to the canvas. Jim was out cold and I had become the heavyweight champion of the world!

COME OUT FIGHTING

WHEN STEPPING into the ring, you should be relaxed and know that you are in the best physical condition possible. Always try to use your head and never become excited. Don't underrate your opponent; but have enough self-confidence to know that you are just as tough as he is. Remember to keep your balance at all times, as it is very easy to be knocked out when off balance. Let each punch count and always punch through and not at your object.

Although it is impossible for anyone to give the various situations which may confront a boxer in the ring, there are a few that can usually be expected.

If you are boxing a tall opponent, try to draw his left lead, then slip inside and start infighting.

Some opponents use only one blow, chiefly a left jab. By side-stepping and weaving, get in close and deliver hard body blows to weaken him.

Sidestepping is also used when your opponent leads with a straight left to your heart. Step outside of it, and bending your body forward, counter with a left to his stomach. Then return to the proper stance.

If boxing a short hitter, you jab and step back; a long swinger, you should step inside to punch.

There are some blows which seem to naturally follow others, such as the straight right following the left jab; and the left hook following the straight right.

Since each opponent has a different style, it is necessary to "feel" him out and discover which blows will effect him more than others. Remember every blow is not a knockout blow; but it can be just as effective because each blow can be used to weaken your opponent, so that he will only need one more to finish him.

Remember there are thirteen fouls a boxer will be penalized for, they are:

1 — Hitting below the belt.

2 — Hitting an opponent while he is down or while getting up after being down.

3 — Holding an opponent or deliberately holding a clinch.

4 — Hitting with the inside or butt of the hand, wrist or elbow.

5 — Holding with one hand, hitting with the other.

6 — Using the kidney punch (hitting deliberately the part of the body over the kidneys).

7 — Using the pivot (a blow delivered by swinging completely around) or rabbit punch (a blow to the back of the neck usually dealt with the side of the hand).

8 — Using abusive or profane language.

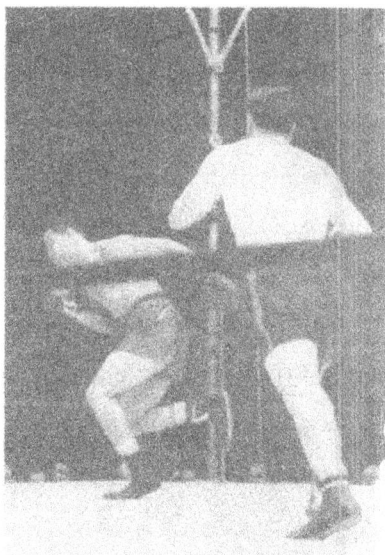

TAMI MAURIELLO HAD HIS MOMENT OF
GLORY AFTER HIS FIRST BLOW IN OUR
BOUT IN SEPTEMBER, 1946. IT SHOOK ME
UP, AS THE PHOTO AT RIGHT SHOWS. BUT
I CAME OUT OF IT QUICKLY AND YOU CAN
SEE WHAT HAPPENED AFTER THAT IN THE
OTHER PHOTOS. TAMI BUCKLED UP UNDER
A LEFT HOOK AFTER ONLY TWO MINUTES
AND NINE SECONDS OF THAT FIRST
ROUND, ENDING MY SECOND SHORTEST
HEAVYWEIGHT CHAMPIONSHIP BOUT — TO
DATE. (THE SECOND SCHMELING BOUT
LASTED TWO MINUTES, FOUR SECONDS.)

9   Hitting or flicking with the open glove.

10   Wrestling or roughing on the ropes.

11   Going down without being hit.

12   Butting with the head or shoulders; hitting with the knee.

13   Failure to obey the referee after being warned.

Remember boxing is a sport in which two athletes are trying to outwit each other by use of their muscles; but also remember to respect your opponent and play fair. So break clean and come out fighting!

WHEN A FIGHT IS OVER, I DON'T HAVE ANY GRUDGES. THIS IS TOMMY FARR AND ME AFTER MY FIRST TITLE DEFENCE, I 1937.

JOE LOUIS' TITLE DEFENCES

Aug. 30, 1937........TOMMY FARR...........15 rds. decision
Feb. 23, 1938........NATHAN MANN........ 3 rounds K.O.
April 1, 1938........HARRY THOMAS........ 5 rounds K.O.
June 22, 1938........MAX SCHMELING....... 1 round K.O.
Jan. 23, 1939........JOHN HENRY LEWIS.... 1 round K.O.
April 17, 1939........JACK ROPER .... 1 round K.O.
June 28, 1939........TONY GALENTO........ 4 rounds K.O.
Sept. 20, 1939........BOB PASTOR...........11 rounds K.O.
Feb. 9, 1940........ARTURO GODOY........15 rds. decision
Mar. 29, 1940........JOHNNY PAYCHEK ..... 2 rounds K.O.
June 20, 1940........ARTURO GODOY....... 8 rounds K.O.
Dec. 16, 1940........AL McCOY.............. 6 rounds K.O.
Jan. 31, 1941........RED BURMAN.......... 5 rounds K.O.
Feb. 17, 1941........GUS DORAZIO .... 2 rounds K.O.
Mar. 21, 1941........ABE SIMON.............13 rounds K.O.
April 8, 1941........TONY MUSTO .... 9 rounds K.O
May 23, 1941........BUDDY BAER .... 7 rounds K.O.
June 18, 1941........BILLY CONN ....13 rounds K.O.
Sept. 29, 1941........LOU NOVA .... 6 rounds K.O.
Jan. 9, 1942........BUDDY BAER .... 1 round K.O.
Mar. 27, 1942........ABE SIMON............. 6 rounds K.O.
June, 19, 1946........BILLY CONN............ 8 rounds K.O.
Sept. 18, 1946........TAMI MAURIELLO...... 1 round K.O.
Dec. 5, 1947........JOE WALCOTT...........15 rds. decision
June 28, 1948........JOE WALCOTT...........11 rounds K.O.

HEAVYWEIGHT CHAMPIONS OF THE WORLD

(Under Marquis of Queensbury rules)

JAMES J. CORBETT	1892–1897
ROBERT L. FITZSIMMONS	1897–1899
JAMES J. JEFFRIES	(ret.) 1899–1905
MARVIN HART	1905–1906
TOMMY BURNS	1906–1908
JACK JOHNSON	1908–1915
JESS WILLARD	1915–1919
JACK DEMPSEY	1919–1926
GENE TUNNEY	(ret.) 1926–1928
MAX SCHMELING	1930–1931
JACK SHARKEY	1932–1933
PRIMO CARNERA	1933–1934
MAX BAER	1934–1935
JAMES J. BRADDOCK	1935–1937
JOE LOUIS	1937

LIGHT HEAVYWEIGHT CHAMPIONS

(161-175 lbs.)

GEORGE GARDNER	1903–1903
BOB FITZSIMMONS	1903–1905
PHILA. JACK O'BRIEN	1905–1907
TOMMY BURNS	1907–1913
JACK DILLON	1913–1916
BATTLING LEVINSKY	1916–1920
GEORGES CARPENTIER	1920–1922
GENE TUNNEY	1922–1922
BATTLING SIKI	1922–1923

MIKE McTIGUE.................................... 1923–1925
PAUL BERLENBACH 1925–1926
JACK DELANEY 1926–1927
TOMMY LOUGHRAN 1927–1929
MAX ROSENBLOOM 1930–1934
BOB OLIN... 1934–1935
JOHN HENRY LEWIS............................. 1935–1938
MELIO BETTINA 1939–1939
BILLY CONN................................ (res.) 1939–1941
ANTON CHRISTOFORIDIS........................ 1941–1941
GUS LESNEVICH................................. 1941–1948
FREDDIE MILLS 1948

MIDDLEWEIGHT CHAMPIONS
(160 lbs.)

JACK DEMPSEY................................... 1884–1891
BOB FITZSIMMONS 1891–1896
STANLEY KETCHEL............................... 1907–1907
BILLY PARKE..................................... 1907–1908
STANLEY KETCHEL .... (died) 1908–1910
FRANK KLAUS 1913–1913
GEORGE CHIP 1913–1914
AL McCOY 1914–1917
MIKE O'DOWD................................... 1917–1920
JOHNNY WILSON............................... 1920–1923
HARRY GREB.................................... 1923–1926
TIGER FLOWERS................................. 1926–1926
MICKEY WALKER 1926–1931
LOU BROUILLARD................................ 1931–1933
VINCE DUNDEE.................................. 1933–1934
TEDDY YAROSZ 1934–1935
BABE RISKO 1935–1936
FREDDY STEELE................................. 1936–1938

```
AL  HOSTAK.......................................  1938–1940
CEFERINO  GARCIA.......................  (N.Y.) 1939–1940
TONY  ZALE..............................  (N.B.A.) 1940
KEN  OVERLIN...........................  (N.Y.) 1940–1941
BILLY  SOOSE..............................  (res.) 1941–1941
TONY  ZALE.......................................  1941–1947
ROCKY  GRAZIANO.............................  1947–1948
TONY  ZALE.......................................  1948–1948
MARCEL  CERDAN .............................  1948
```

WELTERWEIGHT CHAMPIONS
(147 lbs.)

```
BILLY SMITH ....................................  1892–1894
TOMMY RYAN.....................................  1894–1897
BILLY SMITH ....................................  1897–1900
RUBE FERNS......................................  1900–1900
MATTY MATTHEWS ............................  1900–1901
RUBE FERNS......................................  1901–1901
JOE WALCOTT ...................................  1901–1906
HONEY MELODY .................................  1906–1907
MIKE SULLIVAN..................................  1907–1910
JIMMY CLABBY...................................  1910–1911
TED LEWIS.......................................  1915–1919
JACK BRITTON ..................................  1919–1922
MICKEY WALKER ...............................  1922–1926
PETE LATZO .....................................  1926–1927
JOE DUNDEE ....................................  1927–1929
JACKIE FIELDS .................................  1929–1930
JACK THOMPSON................................  1930–1930
TOMMY FREEMAN .............................  1930–1931
JACK THOMPSON................................  1931–1931
LOU BROUILLARD..............................  1931–1932
```

JACKIE FIELDS	1932–1933
YOUNG CORBETT	1933–1933
JIMMY McLARNIN	1933–1934
BARNEY ROSS	1934–1934
JIMMY McLARNIN	1934–1935
BARNEY ROSS	1935–1938
HENRY ARMSTRONG	1938–1940
FRITZIE ZIVIC	1940–1941
FREDDIE COCHRANE	1941–1944
MARTY SERVO	1944–1946
RAY ROBINSON	1946

LIGHTWEIGHT CHAMPIONS
(135 lbs.)

JACK McAULIFFE		1885–1893
KID LAVIGNE		1893–1899
FRANK ERNE		1899–1901
JOE GANS		1901–1908
BATTLING NELSON		1908–1910
AD WOLGAST		1910–1912
WILLIE RITCHIE		1912–1914
FREDDIE WELSH		1914–1917
BENNY LEONARD	(ret.)	1917–1924
JIMMY GOODRICH		1925–1925
ROCKY KANSAS		1925–1926
SAMMY MANDELL		1926–1930
AL SINGER		1930–1930
TONY CANZONERI		1930–1933
BARNEY ROSS	(res.)	1933–1935
TONY CANZONERI		1935–1936
LOU AMBERS		1936–1938
HENRY ARMSTRONG	(res.)	1938–1939

LEW JENKINS...................................... 1940–1941
SAMMY ANGOTT............................ (res.) 1941–1942
BEAU JACK....................................... 1942–1943
BOB MONTGOMERY............................. 1943-1943
BEAU JACK....................................... 1943-1944
SAMMY ANGOTT.........................(N.B.A.) 1943–1944
BOB MONTGOMERY........................ (N.Y.) 1944
IKE WILLIAMS............................. (N.B.A.) 1945

FEATHERWEIGHT CHAMPIONS
(126 lbs.) (from 1937)

HENRY ARMSTRONG........................ (res.) 1937–1938
JOEY ARCHIBALD 1938–1940
HENRY JAFFRA 1940–1941
CHALKY WRIGHT 1941–1942
WILLIE PEP 1942-1948
SANDY SADDLER 1948

BANTAMWEIGHT CHAMPIONS
(118 lbs.) (from 1937)

HENRY JAFFRA 1937–1938
SIXTO ESCOBAR .... (res.) 1938–1940
GEORGE PACE.................................... 1941–1941
LOU SALICA 1941–1942
MANUEL ORTIZ 1942

FLYWEIGHT CHAMPIONS
(112 lbs.) (from 1937)

BENNY LYNCH .... (res.) 1937–1938
PETER KANE..................................(ret.) 1938–1943
JACKIE PATERSON.............................. 1943–1948
RINTY MONOGHAN 1948

WELL, SO LONG, FOLKS. HOPE I'LL ALWAYS BE A WINNER IN YOUR ESTEEM.

www.ingramcontent.com/pod-product-compliance
Lightning Source LLC
Chambersburg PA
CBHW070827100426
42813CB00003B/525